What Makes Me A
UNITARIAN?

Morgan E. Hughes

KIDHAVEN PRESS
An imprint of Thomson Gale, a part of The Thomson Corporation

Detroit • New York • San Francisco • San Diego • New Haven, Conn.
Waterville, Maine • London • Munich

For more information, contact
KidHaven Press
27500 Drake Rd.
Farmington Hills, MI 48331-3535
Or you can visit our Internet site at http://www.gale.com

LIBRARY OF CONGRESS CATALOGING-IN-PUBLICATION DATA

Hughes, Morgan, 1957—
    Unitarian / by Morgan E. Hughes.
        p. cm. — (What makes me a— ?)
    Includes bibliographical references and index.
    ISBN 0-7377-3181-8 (alk. paper)
    1. Unitarian Universalist Association. 2. Unitarian Universalist churches. 3. Unitarians.
    4. Universalists. I. Title. II. Series.
    BX9841.3.H84 2005
    289.1—dc22
                                                                            2005009011

Printed in the United States of America

CONTENTS

CHAPTER ONE

How Did My Religion Begin?

Unitarianism was first introduced in the 1500s by a group of Christian scholars in central Europe. They had studied the *Bible* carefully and decided that some church teaching of the time was wrong. They concluded that the scriptures contained no evidence of a Holy Trinity; that is, God as the Father, the Son, and the Holy Spirit. These scholars believed, just as Jesus had, in only one God. So they called themselves Unitarians. Later, they were joined by others who felt that this God loved all humans equally, that hell did not exist as the orthodox Christian church said it did, and that salvation was for everyone, or universal. These groups came together and became known as Unitarian Universalists.

In addition to their belief in one God instead of the Trinity, Unitarian Universalists differ from other traditional orthodox Christians. One difference is their desire to practice the religion shared by Jesus, not to participate in a religion *about* Jesus. Unitarian Universalists also hold that a sincere commitment (**covenant**) is more important and meaningful than a strict list of beliefs (**creeds**).

A Religion of Many Beliefs

Modern Unitarian Universalism is known for embracing many different beliefs. A typical Unitarian Universalist worship service might include people from many religious traditions (Jewish, Christian, **Buddhist**, **Muslim**, **atheist**, or **agnostic**). Most importantly, Unitarian Universalists share a commitment to practice their religion freely. They worship together, sing and pray together, study and teach together, and work for social justice together. Still, each person can hold his or her personal beliefs.

Holding hands, a congregation of Unitarian Universalists sings during a worship service.

Today, most of the world's Unitarian Universalists live in the United States, with about 600,000 divided among 1,000 or so **congregations**. In Europe, there are still about 100,000 Hungarian-speaking Unitarians in 200 churches in Romania and Hungary. In addition, about 200 or so small Unitarian Universalist congregations exist in Great Britain and Ireland, with another 30 in Canada, 35 in India, and several scattered among 20 other nations around the world. All of these congregations are associated through the International Council of Unitarians and Universalists.

A History of Persecution

Even though it has always been known for its welcoming acceptance of all people, Unitarianism was not accepted when it first emerged. Because it rejected the existence of the Holy Trinity, Unitarianism and those who practiced it often faced severe criticism from the leaders of orthodox Christian churches.

In central Europe in the 16th century, early Unitarians were frequent victims of harsh **persecution**. For example, Michael Servetus was a Spanish doctor and philosopher who had trained under a Franciscan monk. When he wrote that biblical scriptures did not support the claim of a Holy Trinity, he was convicted of **heresy** and burned at the stake. He would not be the last to die for his faith.

Unitarianism spread gradually from central Europe to Great Britain. In the 1600s, an English biblical scholar named John Biddle wrote an article entitled "Twelve

In 1553 Michael Servetus, one of the first Unitarians, was burned alive for not believing in the Holy Trinity.

Arguments Drawn Out of Scriptures." In it, he echoed previous Unitarian writers with a dismissal of the Holy Trinity. Biddle went even further, accusing leaders of the orthodox Christian church of social and economic corruption. He accused them of ignoring the needs of the poor and of using their power to keep the people in line. Like Servetus, he was convicted of heresy. He escaped execution, but spent much of his life in jail.

Unitarianism in America

In America at the time of the American Revolution, many of the Founding Fathers were practicing Unitarians, including John Adams and Thomas Jefferson. The most respected leader of the time was a Boston minister named William Ellery Channing. In 1819, at the ordination of the First Independent Church in Baltimore, Maryland, Chan-

William Ellery Channing, a nineteenth-century Unitarian preacher, believed in free thinking and social change.

ning delivered an historic sermon called "Unitarian Christianity." In it, he outlined ideals of Unitarianism as it prepared to move forward. He spoke of the importance of free speech, education reform, peace, justice, relief for the poor, women's rights, and the abolition of slavery. He also proposed that everyone had a right to think and worship in his or her own way.

Channing concluded:

> Our earnest prayer to God is, . . . HE shall come, whose right it is to rule the minds of men; that the conspiracy of ages against the liberty of Christians may be brought to an end; that the servile assent, so long yielded to human creeds, may give place to honest and devout inquiry into the Scriptures; and that Christianity, thus purified from error, may put forth its almighty energy, and prove itself, by its ennobling influence on the mind, to be indeed "the power of God unto salvation."[1]

Throughout the 19th century, Unitarianism continued to expand. Poet Ralph Waldo Emerson, a follower of Channing and a trained minister, spoke about the value of science and scientific discovery. He also encouraged Unitarians to explore and embrace such Eastern religions as **Shintoism** and **Hinduism**. This was a noteworthy step because it helped promote the Universalist elements of Unitarianism. Today, Unitarian Universalists accept all religious traditions and view advances in scientific discovery as a complement—not a contradiction—to their faith.

Modern Unitarians are very tolerant of other religions and their gods, including the Hindu goddess Parvati.

Many others made important contributions to the growth of Unitarianism. One such man was Theodore Parker, a New England scholar in the 1800s. While Parker was too poor to attend Harvard, he was bright enough to read the school's entire curriculum on his own. He wrote about something he called divine inspiration. While he shared the Unitarian vision of Jesus as a human being inspired by God, and not the literal son of God, Parker also maintained that God was fully present

Unitarian minister Theodore Parker preached that God was fully present in all people and things.

in all matter and in all people. He advanced the idea that any man or woman was capable—indeed worthy—of being inspired by God, just as Jesus had been.

Modern Unitarian Universalists continue to base their faith on the simple idea that it is God's will that all human beings must be free to hear what they call the inner summons of conscience. In other words, humans must listen to the voice inside that tells them the difference between right and wrong. Unitarian Universalists hold that it is wrong to deny any individual his or her religious freedom and that to do so would turn God into a tyrant. Such an approach would spoil the notion of the loving God who gives all people their dignity and value.

CHAPTER TWO

What Do I Believe?

L ike many mainstream religions, Unitarian Universalism follows certain agreed-upon principles, or guiding rules. These fall into seven specific areas. Unitarians covenant, or promise,

> to affirm and promote (1) the inherent worth and dignity of every person; (2) justice, equality and compassion in human relations; (3) acceptance of one another; (4) a free and responsible search for truth and meaning; (5) the right of conscience and the use of the democratic process within our congregations and in society at large; (6) the goal of world community with peace, liberty, and justice for all; and (7) respect for the interdependent web of all existence of which we are a part.[2]

Throughout their history, it has been the practice of Unitarians to celebrate the equality of all people, regardless

Unitarians believe that all people are equal regardless of their sex or race.

of race, creed, sex, or religion. Unitarians strongly reject any class or caste system that puts one group of people above another based on economic privilege or traditional social standing. For example, according to Unitarian belief, a rich man is no better than a poor man just because he has more money. Both people are of equal fundamental worth. Unitarians oppose all forms of discrimination and believe there is no place for violence in a civilized society, whether it is committed by citizens or by governing authorities.

Thus, Unitarians hold a basic acceptance of each person on the strength of his or her inherent worth (or

Unitarians are strong supporters of scientific research, including stem cell research (pictured).

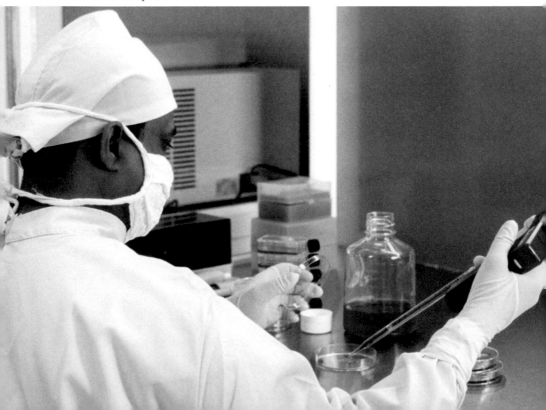

inborn value). Unitarians also believe there can be—must be—a strong link between science and religious development. This holds for all scientific thought (which may include everything from Darwin's theory of evolution to current work in such **controversial** fields as stem cell research). These scientific breakthroughs go hand in hand with Unitarians' desire to live fully as humans and do not conflict with their wish to explore the religions of the world. Discoveries in science, for

Unitarians emphasize the importance of community service. Here, Unitarian teens serve Christmas dinner at a homeless shelter.

example, in no way negate or diminish religious or spiritual growth, or vice versa.

This is possible, in part, because Unitarians do not subscribe to traditional images of God. For example, they do not envision God as a white-bearded grandfather figure sitting on a cloud in the sky. Nor is God seen as some kind of all-powerful super magician who oversees all things great and small, controlling all events good and bad. Unitarians are much more likely to define God in terms of a reverence (respect) for life, the spirit of love or truth, the holy, or the gracious. Unitarians use this kind of language because they feel it is more inclusive. It can be used appropriately both by those who believe in God (theists) as well as by those who perhaps do not believe in God (nontheists or atheists).

Unitarians and Jesus

Along these lines, Unitarians also have a different view of Jesus. Many Christian faiths hold that Jesus was literally the divine son of God. Unitarians do not agree. Instead, they embrace Jesus as a God-filled human being, not a supernatural being. Unitarians still revere Jesus, and Jesus remains a powerful symbol of unconditional love and enormous sacrifice. He maintains an honored place among the great prophets and teachers who came out of the Jewish tradition. Today's Unitarians place Jesus in the same category of such highly respected, highly cherished leaders and teachers as Moses and Buddha.

For Unitarians, salvation is closely connected with the vision of Jesus as a God-filled man, rather than as a

Unitarians respect Jesus Christ (left) as an extraordinary teacher in the same way they honor Buddha (below).

divine figure. The word *salvation* comes from the Latin word *salus,* meaning health. Unitarians do not view salvation as something given only to those who live a moral life and who are eventually washed clean of their sins. Instead, they see salvation as a kind of spiritual health or wholeness. Salvation is more closely related to personal growth, the pursuit of wisdom, the strength of one's character, the gift of insight, understanding, inner and outer peace, courage, patience, and compassion. All of these things can have significant healing powers.

Views of the *Bible*

Like other Christians, Unitarians study the *Bible*. And because it is recognized and accepted as a sacred text, the *Bible* receives the same respect and honor as, for example, the **Torah** receives from faithful Hebrews. It is used to instruct children in Sunday school and in summertime *Bible* camps. Unitarians especially cherish the

Although Unitarians are devoted to studying the *Bible*, they do not interpret its teachings literally.

prophets (Amos, Hosea, Isaiah, and others) because these brave souls dared to speak words that were critical of those who held power. These prophets called for social justice and equality and challenged religious authorities even when it was dangerous to do so. Unitarians do not believe the *Bible* is infallible (that is, without mistakes, contradictions, or errors) or that it should be used as the only source of truth. Unitarians believe the *Bible* should be read with the same critical, questioning approach one would take when reading anything from a daily newspaper to a work of modern or classical fiction, with an eye toward finding truth and understanding.

In their religious studies, both children and adults study a variety of holy scriptures. In addition to examining text from the Christian *Bible,* they also give respectful consideration to passages from ancient sources, including the *Torah* of Hebrew faith and the **Koran** (the holy book of the Islamic prophet Muhammad).

Most Unitarians seek social justice and embrace all of mankind. They also view the pursuit of truth and understanding as one of the most important aspects of their faith journey.

CHAPTER THREE

How Do I Practice My Faith?

Because of their strong desire to maintain their sense of spiritual independence, Unitarians differ from many mainstream Christians. For example, Unitarian congregations are not required to follow the lead of a higher church authority, such as a bishop. Each congregation may run the church themselves, set their own agenda for study and worship, and choose whomever they please to serve as their minister. Of course, as with any of the mainstream religions, Unitarian ministers are fully trained and approved through accepted seminary programs.

Despite their many significant differences, Unitarians also share some important characteristics with other Christian faiths. For example, their worship services are held on Sundays in a standard church setting. They include many recognizable elements. Hymns are sung from the Unitarian **hymnal**, called *Singing the Living*

During a worship service, Unitarian congregations sing hymns from their hymnal, *Singing the Living Tradition.*

Tradition. This hymnal differs from traditional Christian hymnals mostly in terms of its more modern, gender-inclusive language. For example, God is not referred to as "him" or "he" in a Unitarian hymnal. Unitarian services also include a sermon, a time for congregants to share joys and concerns with their fellow worshippers, and the lighting of the **chalice**.

The chalice is the physical symbol of Unitarianism. At the start of each worship service, the chalice is lit. The chalice itself represents sharing, generosity, and love—the "cup of plenty," as it were. The flame represents, among other things, witness, illumination, sacrifice, and courage. The symbol originated during World War II, when the Unitarian Service Committee (USC) was founded to assist war refugees who needed to escape Nazi persecution. An artist named Hans Deutsch drew the flaming chalice in 1941 so that the USC could mark its official documents. Later, the director of the USC, Charles Joy, said: "It represents . . . the kind of chalice the Greeks and Romans put on their altars. The holy oil burning is a symbol of our helpfulness and sacrifice."[3]

Sermons

Unitarian sermons, which are typically delivered by the senior minister but may also be given by a layperson on occasion, tend to address universal topics and themes. They are not required to—and as a rule do not—follow a standard **lectionary**. The lectionary is a kind of guide, established by each **denomination** (for example, Lutheran, United Church of Christ, Methodist, and Episcopalian), that sets a schedule of scripture study. This ensures that any number of churches within a single denomination will all be using the same scripture readings on any given Sunday. Unitarian ministers frequently preach on themes of life, truth, and meaning. They use stories, myths, poems, and scripture selections from a variety of world religions to illustrate their message.

A Unitarian minister reads aloud from an illustrated *Bible* to children during Sunday school.

While scripture study is an important aspect of the adult worship service, so is the use of Sunday school for youngsters. Children in Unitarian education explore many of the world's religions, comparing and contrasting them with what they have learned about traditional Judeo-Christian faiths. These children are encouraged to think for themselves and to develop their own set of beliefs without strict rules or guidelines. Each study program is determined by members of the local congregation. It may include programs in interpersonal relations, ethics, nature and ecology, heroes and heroines of social reform, the *Bible,* Unitarian Universalist history, and holy days around the world.

Holidays

Unitarians include many traditions in their recognition of holiday celebrations and sacred ceremonies. For example, they enthusiastically observe both Christmas and Passover, as well as the Hindu holiday Divali and the African celebration of Kwanzaa. Each of these traditions

An African American family lights candles during Kwanzaa, one of the holidays celebrated by Unitarians.

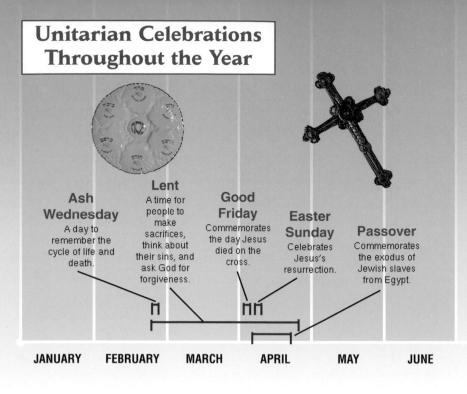

Unitarian Celebrations Throughout the Year

Ash Wednesday
A day to remember the cycle of life and death.

Lent
A time for people to make sacrifices, think about their sins, and ask God for forgiveness.

Good Friday
Commemorates the day Jesus died on the cross.

Easter Sunday
Celebrates Jesus's resurrection.

Passover
Commemorates the exodus of Jewish slaves from Egypt.

JANUARY FEBRUARY MARCH APRIL MAY JUNE

is celebrated in a universal context, with no extra emphasis given to one over the other. Unitarians conduct weddings, the naming or dedicating of children (which is similar in some ways to Christian baptism), and **memorializing** the deceased, always using simple, modern, inclusive language.

Since Unitarian Universalists come from many different backgrounds, there is quite a bit of traditional celebration among them. Early Unitarians in America contributed many carols and customs to the celebration of Christmas. These Unitarians did not agree with the Puritan tradition of ignoring the holiday. Today, Unitarians from mainstream Christian faiths may freely observe all the traditions of Christmas, complete with decorated trees, carol singing (a very popular Unitarian activity), and the exchange of gifts.

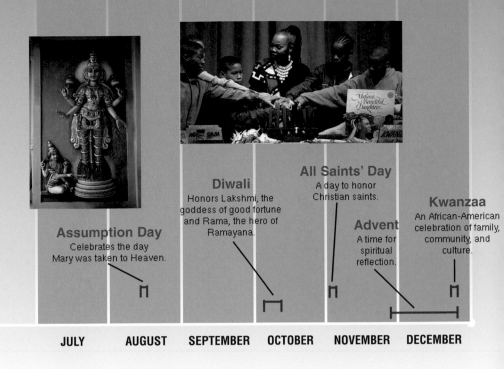

Assumption Day
Celebrates the day Mary was taken to Heaven.

Diwali
Honors Lakshmi, the goddess of good fortune and Rama, the hero of Ramayana.

All Saints' Day
A day to honor Christian saints.

Advent
A time for spiritual reflection.

Kwanzaa
An African-American celebration of family, community, and culture.

| JULY | AUGUST | SEPTEMBER | OCTOBER | NOVEMBER | DECEMBER |

Unitarian Universalists in the 21st century can be counted upon to offer an inclusive and interfaith approach to how they observe, interpret, and celebrate many of the world's key holidays. For example, Unitarians often hold community services celebrating Jewish holidays, such as Passover, which celebrates the Exodus of the Jews from Egypt. Hanukkah, which frequently coincides with Christmas, is a celebration of the Jewish victory over the Syrians in 165 B.C. Unitarians welcome the chance to "cross over" and share the special and important traditions practiced by those who come from different faiths.

It is interesting that Easter services are very popular among Unitarians—just as they are among mainstream Christians—even though the focus of the celebration is something that Unitarians do not believe: that Jesus was

Crowds gather at an Easter sunrise service at the Grand Canyon. Easter is a favorite holiday among Unitarians.

resurrected three days after his crucifixion. However, the Easter celebration still holds great meaning for Unitarians. While they do not think that Jesus came back from the dead, they do use this ceremony to connect the "rebirth of Christ" to their belief in the rebirth of the Earth.

Differences from Christianity

Other ceremonies also have great meaning for Unitarians and are used to bring together their faith community. Unitarians are opposed to the doctrine of original sin. They do not agree that ever since the sin of Adam in the Garden of Eden, everyone is born with sin. At the same time, Universalists disagree with the idea of eternal punishment (or going to hell for having lived a sinful life). As a result, Unitarian Universalists do not baptize their children, which in some traditions may be seen as a method of washing away original sin. (In all mainstream Christian traditions, baptism is a sacred rite used to initiate a person—man, woman, or child—into a life of Christianity. It usually includes a promise to live by the teachings of Jesus Christ.) Instead, Unitarians welcome their youngsters in a service of dedication, sometimes called the naming of children.

The Naming of a Child

The naming of a child is a service which takes place during the course of a regular Sunday worship service. The service itself is usually quite short. Most services center upon a baby or very young toddler but, on occasion, a service is held for an older child or young adult. In it, a youngster is joined by one or both parents before the congregation. While the ceremony differs by congregation, there is a common theme among most naming of a child services. The congregation—the youngster's faith family—is asked if it will do everything in its power to support, encourage, and nurture the child's spiritual growth. The congregation then affirms that it will do so, usually with a unison response of "We will." The minister may then sprinkle water on a rose and use this to anoint (or bless) the child and bring him or her officially into the community of faith.

At adolescence, many teenage congregants become involved in a coming of age program and ceremony. This is similar to the confirmation process popular in mainstream Christian faiths and the bar mitzvah services conducted in the Jewish faith.

Unitarian Universalist rites of passage—such as the marriage ceremony—are an important aspect of church life. Unitarian ministers usually work closely with couples who are planning a wedding ceremony. Together, they try to create a service that is personal and represents the people as individuals, a service that reflects their unique family backgrounds, values, and shared aspirations. The bride and groom have a great deal of input in this process and are encouraged to shape the service to their liking.

Memorial services in Unitarian Universalist practice are somewhat different than traditional funeral services. As with all services, Unitarian ministers work closely with families and loved ones. Together, they work to produce a service that is realistic about death and grief but also strives to celebrate joyfully the life that has ended.

CHAPTER FOUR

What Is the Future of Unitarianism?

There is good news for Unitarian Universalists worldwide. After several hundred years that were often marked by struggle and persecution, this open and embracing faith is thriving the world over. There are currently more than 1,000 congregations in the United States and Canada alone. These congregations are associated with the Unitarian Universalist Association (UUA). North American Unitarian Universalists have ties with other Unitarian Universalist congregations in other parts of the world as well, through their membership in an organization called the International Association for Religious Freedom (IARF). IARF was founded more than 100 years ago. The IARF is a registered charity based in the United Kingdom that has the aim of working for freedom of religion and belief at a global level. They have a lot in common with Unitarians. They encourage interfaith dialogue and **tolerance** and are proud of more than 100 years of experience

A Unitarian Universal minister in Virginia leads his congregation in prayer outside the church.

in this work. In addition to its connections with Unitarians worldwide, the IARF also has affiliations with Humanist, Hindu Reform, Shinto, and Buddhist groups (as do Unitarians).

The world's oldest Unitarian congregations are still in Romania. This is the actual birthplace of Unitarianism. In recent years, there has been a strong movement to reestablish the Unitarian church in this region of central Europe.

Large groups of Unitarians also live in the Khasi Hills of India, as well as in Australia, South Africa, France, Great Britain, Poland, Germany, and the Czech Republic. Thanks to the work of tireless **missionaries**, Unitarian churches and congregations may also be found in such Asia-Pacific nations as Japan and the Philippines.

Unitarianism in the United States Today

Here in the United States, steps are continually taken to make sure the Unitarian Universalism stays fresh and focused on its open and welcoming principles. Sometimes

A gay couple exchanges marriage vows in a Unitarian church in Massachusetts. Unitarians support same-sex marriage.

the developments are quite controversial, but that does not stop the forward movement. In 1970 the UUA passed a resolution which called for an end to all discrimination against homosexuals and bisexuals. Three years later, in 1973, the UUA's general assembly voted to create the Office of Gay Affairs. Its name was later changed to the Office of Bisexual, Gay, Lesbian and Transgender Concerns. Currently, the UUA is the only religious organization that is

In 2001 William Sinkford became the first African American president of the Unitarian Universal Association.

completely **open and affirming** when it comes to recognizing and accepting gay, lesbian, and transgender issues (such as same-sex marriage and gay ministers).

Common Concern

In 2001 the UUA elected William Sinkford to serve as president of their organization. He was the seventh person to hold this prestigious office, and the first African American. Beliefnet, a multifaith electronic site, recently named Reverend Sinkford to its list of the nation's most prominent and powerful African American religious leaders.

Hand in hand with their desire to worship freely, Unitarians the world over are currently redoubling their efforts to form a stronger, more all-embracing association of churches. With this objective in mind, Unitarians continue to rely heavily on education and open discussion as tools to forge the personal and spiritual growth of every individual. Unitarians all over the world share a common concern not only for their own little corner of the globe, but for people and issues everywhere. Among the areas of specific focus facing Unitarians in the 21st century are youth ministries, social justice, peace, and political freedom.

In 2005 a study of over 100,000 first-year college students in the United States showed a high interest in spirituality, broad tolerance for religious freedom, and a desire for spiritual growth among students surveyed. The study, conducted by the Higher Education Research Institute, found that large majorities of first-year students have an interest in spirituality (80 percent) and are searching for meaning and purpose in their lives (76 percent). Of particular note was the study's findings regarding Unitarian Universalist students. According to the study, students naming Unitarian Universalist as their religious choice had the highest response scores on measures of spiritual searching, volunteer service, social justice work, caring for others, and interest in/respect for different religious viewpoints.

Unitarian Universalism continues to inspire great acts. In the spring of 2005, the UUA received a record-setting 2.1 million dollar bequest—an inheritance—from minister and hospice chaplain Reverend Arthur Reublinger. The gift was announced during the UUA's New Hampshire/Vermont district meeting in Portsmouth's South Church in April 2005. This extraordinary act of generosity is the largest single gift the UUA has ever received. It is to be used to support special programming for a specific region of the country and will establish the Arthur H. Reublinger Small Church Ministries Endowment Fund. The fund will provide resources to help strengthen small congregations throughout the district.

This gift points to the power of one person's dream and demonstrates how a single act of generosity can ripple out into the world to benefit those of us here and now and those yet to come.

People of Action

There is an old adage that suggests that a man or woman of words and not of deeds is like a garden full of weeds. That is to say, it is far more important to be measured by what one does than by what one merely says. Throughout

A group of Unitarian college students takes time from their busy day to study the *Bible* together.

the years, Unitarians have always made it an essential goal to help bring about much needed change and social reform around the world, not with flowery speeches and heated **rhetoric** but with concrete action. Through their coordinated efforts under the leadership of the UUA, Unitarians have always operated under the idea of being people of deeds and not of creeds. The only oath Unitarians swear to is the oath to remain open-minded and welcoming to all people, regardless of any differences that may exist.

Unitarianism has always been, and will always be, a "do-it-yourself" faith. The only requirement of any person

These members of a Unitarian youth group in Vermont raised a large sum of money to donate to an environmental group in Costa Rica.

to be a faithful Unitarian is that one must agree to work at it, to use not only the heart and soul, but the mind as well. In other words, Unitarian Universalists seek to act as a moral force in the world, believing that ethical living is the supreme witness of religion. The here and now—and the effects their actions will have on future generations— deeply concern them. They believe their relationships with one another, with diverse peoples, races, and nations, should be governed—first and foremost—by justice, equity, and compassion.

NOTES

Chapter 1: How Did Unitarianism Begin?

1. William E. Channing, "Unitarian Christianity," The Transcendentalists. www.transcendentalists.com/unitarian _christianity.htm.

Chapter 2: What Do Unitarians Believe?

2. Unitarian Universalist Association Principles and Purposes. www.uua.org/aboutuua/principles.html.

Chapter 3: How Do Unitarians Practice Their Faith?

3. Quoted in Marshall Hawkins, *"Frequently Asked Questions,"* Unitarian Universalist Association. www.uua.org/ aboutuu/newcomerfaq.html#8.

GLOSSARY

atheist: A person who believes that there is no God.

agnostic: A person who believes that nothing is known or can be known about the existence of God or about things outside of human experience.

Buddhist: A follower of the teachings of Gautama Buddha that teaches that right living will enable people to attain nirvana, the state in which a soul is free from all desire and pain.

chalice: A cup or goblet.

congregations: Groups of people gathered for religious worship.

controversial: A setting in which strong opposing views are present.

covenant: A solemn agreement between two or more persons or groups.

creeds: Brief statements of the essential points of religious belief as approved by some churches.

denomination: The name of a class or group.

heresy: A belief different from the accepted belief of a church, school, profession, or other group.

Hinduism: The religious and social system of the Hindus, a development of ancient Brahmanism. The caste system and the worship of many gods are parts of Hinduism.

hymnal: A church's book of songs (hymns).

Koran: The sacred book of the Muslims. It consists of revelations of Allah to the prophet Muhammad and is the standard by which Muslims regulate their lives. The book, written in Arabic after Muhammad's death, is divided into 114 chapters.

lectionary: A book containing lessons or portions of scripture read at divine service, or a list of passages appointed to be read at worship services.

memorializing: Holding a church service in which one who has died is remembered.

missionaries: Those who are sent to perform charitable or religious work in a foreign country.

Muslim: A follower of Muhammad; believer in Islam, the religion founded by him.

open and affirming: A policy of acceptance, specifically related to gay and lesbian individuals.

persecution: Harassment or oppression by ill treatment.

rhetoric: Verbal communication, words.

Shintoism: The native religion of Japan, primarily the worship of nature deities and of ancestors.

Torah: The body of Jewish teachings and traditions, including the *Talmud* and later rabbinical commentaries and codes.

tolerance: Accepting the thoughts and beliefs of others, even if they are different.

FOR FURTHER EXPLORATION

Books

Victoria Sherrow, *Freedom to Worship*. Brookfield, CT: Millbrook Press, 1997. This book explores the freedom of worship as it is guaranteed in the Bill of Rights, along with its history and important notes.

Stephen J. Stein, *Alternative American Religion*. New York: Oxford University Press, 2000. This book looks at various alternative religions that have existed in the United States since colonial times.

Videorecording

Ashleigh V. Denneth, *What Is Religion?* Wyneewood, PA: Schlessinger Media, 2003. Students learn that, despite their many differences, world religions have elements in common, like systems of belief, holy writings, sacred places, and special holidays and celebrations.

Web Sites

Beliefnet (www.beliefnet.com). Beliefnet is a multifaith e-community designed to help people meet their own religious and spiritual needs in an interesting, captivating, and engaging way.

Fact Monster (www.factmonster.com). This site offers an encylopedia-style resource as well as links to other sites with information on Unitarianism and other world religions.

Family Internet (http://familyinternet.about.com/cs/religion). This site provides articles and resources on a variety of religions and offers links to other sites for children to continue their exploration of religions of the world.

Unitarian Universalist Association (www.uua.org). This is the official site of the UUA and contains lots of useful historical information as well as up-to-the-minute articles on the important issues facing Unitarians in the 21st century.

INDEX

PICTURE CREDITS

ABOUT THE AUTHOR

Morgan E. Hughes is a freelance writer and musician who has covered a wide range of subjects during his 25-year career, from the National Hockey League to professional cycling, major league baseball, collegiate tennis, recreational sports for children, and the wide world of halls of fame all over North America. He is also a playwright and novelist, and co-writer of material on a 1999 alternative country CD on which he played the pedal steel guitar. A native of New York city, he currently lives in Connecticut with his wife and two teenagers.